Lose to Win

Lose to Win
...a journey of risking it all to gain it all

Dr. George A. Ashford, Jr.

XULON PRESS

Xulon Press
2301 Lucien Way #415
Maitland, FL 32751
407.339.4217
www.xulonpress.com

© 2019 by Dr. George A. Ashford, Jr

All rights reserved solely by the author. The author guarantees all contents are original and do not infringe upon the legal rights of any other person or work. No part of this book may be reproduced in any form without the permission of the author. The views expressed in this book are not necessarily those of the publisher.

Unless otherwise indicated, Scriptures marked NIV are taken from the HOLY BIBLE, NEW INTERNATIONAL VERSION,. Copyright © 1973, 1978, 1984 by International Bible Society. Used by permission of Zondervan Publishing House. All rights reserved.

Scripture marked MSG are taken from The Message. Published by permission. Originally published by NavPress in English as THE MESSAGE: The Bible in Contemporary Language copyright 2002 by Eugene Peterson. All rights reserved.

Edited by Xulon Press.

Printed in the United States of America.

ISBN-13: 978-1-5456-6964-8

Dedication

This book is dedicated to my loving and supportive wife Olisa, who loved me when I was diagnosed with cancer and the blessing of our two sons, George Adrian, Jr. and Geordan Alexander.

I would like to further dedicate this book the two persons who helped to establish my faith foundation in Jesus Christ my father and mother Presiding Elder George Ashford and Mrs. Rhudene Ashford.

My father was known for his deep voice and strong personality but underneath he had a heart for people and a love for his family. He was big jokester who was famous for his life quotes, he would often tell me "son in order to get along with some folk in this world you have to give them a good dose of let alone."

My mother was a reading teacher and librarian. She was known for baking cakes, pies and making sweet tea. She to had a strong personality. She provided the nurture and foundation that has helped to shape my ministry.

She and my father raised me and my two sisters Vanessa and Valerie in the church, stressing education and self-discipline. We will always be thankful for their love and sacrifice.

Finally my grandmothers Carrie Bowman Reeves and Pearl Leightner Ashford two woman who embodied Godliness, strength, and discipline.

Acknowledgments

No work or book is written in isolation. Certainly not this one as well. Many people and congregations have helped to shape me along the way. My thanks to all.

But most of all I want to thank the Journey United Methodist Church and Silver Hill Memorial United Methodist Church. These two congregations are living examples of what a new faith community can be and what church revitalization can be in an existing congregation.

Life transform, church growth, and revitalization are signs of the witness of the Holy Spirit in these congregations. Overcoming obstacles have made each of them stronger and helped to establish a strong community presence.

Table of Contents

Dedication vii
Acknowledgments ix
Preface: The Journey xiii
Introduction xxi

Chapter 1: No Fear: Risking It All to Gain It All 1
Chapter 2: Make Defeat Your Fuel 21
Chapter 3: Your Best Life .31
Chapter 4: God's Big Payback 45

Appendix I: No Fear 55
A Journey Prayer 75
Final Word 77
About the Author 79

PREFACE

The Journey

In 1993 I was assigned to my first appointment, three small churches yoked together for what was known as a '3 Point Charge'. Looking back, it was more of a challenge than a charge, but charge I did. I charged forward! In the smallest church, average attendance was three persons including the pastor. The second largest church averaged ten persons, while the largest averaged a little over twenty-five. Many of the members would rotate each Sunday to build up attendance at the sister churches.

As a young seminary student, twenty-three years old, I was full of fire, desire and enthusiasm to grow the church. I had more ideas than time to implement.

Each Sunday was an interesting challenge at the smaller locations due to the older buildings and deferred maintenance. Declining membership meant operating on a shoestring budget, dealing with limited resources and a survival mentality.

Looking at all of the hurdles I faced, I still felt there was hope because one of the three churches had a stable building, adequate facilities, and good visibility being located on one of the main access roads in town.

The solution for me was simple. Why struggle operating separately, when together we could do more. As simple as it seemed, the idea would be met with skepticism and reluctance. I was surprised to know that this idea had been discussed by some, but no one dared to make a move, ***to take the risk***. I then decided to have more conversation within each congregation.

After countless conversations with them, what I discovered was a combination of ***frustration*** and ***fear*** from years of church declination and hurt. The result was discouragement and hesitancy from holding on so long to the hope that the current situation would eventually turn around and go back to the way it used to be. Adding on to the fear and frustration was the reality of being financially strapped, from Sunday to Sunday. There was also a fear of moving forward because as far as they could see, the future was not guaranteed. They wanted the church to grow and reach new people, but feared new people might not cherish the sacred music and the traditions of the past that had sustained the church over the years.

Before leaving as their pastor, the smallest church merged with the largest church. Not soon after, all three congregations would eventually merge as one church.

My journey continued in 1995, as I was assigned to my second appointment to a historic church which had existed for more than a century. The community that once supported this historic church had shifted. Membership was in decline, and an inward introverted focus limited the options for the future. Although great pastors served there in the past, it was apparent that the former glory was gone. Once again, ***<u>a spirit of discouragement, frustration, and fear had set in</u>***.

Little be known to us, a blessing was in store for this congregation, which was once known as the pillar church of the community. Due to a downtown revitalization project, they were offered the opportunity to sell the church and relocate. The offer for the current property was a divine gift from God, almost tripling the market value of the property. If there were ever a time that I was skeptical, it was at this moment that I knew without a doubt, that God was in this plan.

As I prayerfully considered the possibilities for the future growth and survival of the church, the options were clear. Sit and wait on a slow death, or ***take risks*** making changes to create something new, perhaps beyond what's been familiar. This would mean intentionally seeking to establish a congregational culture that attracts people, as well as possess a winning spirit, (yes, we can do all things through Christ who strengthens us.) We were ready to send souls out to share the story of Christ within the community. As their pastor, I too was ready to ***lead beyond what was familiar***.

A church meeting was called to decide on the future. On that day the church was full of people, many hoping and expecting something new. However, it was apparent that some were scared and fearful. At the end of the meeting, one of the oldest members of the church stood up and challenged the church. She was an eighty plus years old, former school teacher, who was also blind, and had lived next door to the church for many years. As she stood to speak, her message was loud and clear. She said, "The same God that is taking care of me and giving me the courage to move, will take care of the church to relocate to a new facility." As the old saying goes, after that "church was over"!

As the excitement and momentum continued, in 1998 the church relocated to a new thirty-three thousand square foot facility, and received a ministry grant of one hundred fifty thousand dollars. After relocating, the church experienced exponential growth in worship, allowing us to hire the church's first full-time associate pastor. During this time, the church also purchased a new parsonage. Additionally, our children and youth ministry became a primary focus, along with community involvement, revitalized worship, stewardship, and pastoral stability. The growth of the church, as well as the new additions, can be attributed to the relocation of the church. It was a win, win for everyone. The church continued to grow and thrive, with 500+ in worship each Sunday. This is what can happen when you refuse to let your fears become a factor for progress.

In 2006, I made the transition to a conference staff position as a Congressional Specialist, focusing on African American churches. Although a historic appointment, and the first of its kind in our Annual Conference, what I quickly observed in this position was a desperate need within some churches to grow and revitalize their congregations. In retrospect, I also observed churches that were happy and content to remain just as they were. Although the position was very rewarding my desire was to return to the pulpit.

In 2007 I had the opportunity to start a new church through the process of what is called a parachute drop, literally meaning drop a pastor into a community and establish a new church. Journey Church was started with three other people, my wife and two sons. We began worshipping in an old abandoned warehouse space, and within the first six months, we grew to fifty persons in worship. In the next three years, we would relocate and grow the church to more than two hundred fifty persons.

The journey continues……..Within six years, Journey outgrew its second location and relocated to a middle school for the next three years. Amazingly, during this time, our membership reached five hundred. We were able to purchase eleven acres of land and began making plans to build phase one of Journey Church.

During this time by the grace of God, we would overcome numerous obstacles, including persons leaving the church, burglaries, staff transitions, health challenges and unforeseen opposition. Even with these obstacles, we continued to push for growth and to nurture new members, many of which never belonged to a church prior to Journey. A lot of my time was spent balancing and nurturing the new church, while trying to cast the vision to build and stabilize the congregation. There were many times when details and personal matters within my own life had to be set aside for the greater good of the church. I confronted daily fatigue and to some degree depression while maintaining focus on what needed to be done.

In 2012 construction began on the new facility. The construction process was tedious and arduous as we faced issues with contractors, and dealt with internal issues within the team. Engaging a project of this magnitude is difficult under normal conditions, but in a new church with people who have very little history together working through a building process proved to be challenging. Membership continued to grow reaching beyond 700 persons, and still today continues to grow with close to 1,000 members.

The purpose of this book is twofold:

1. To inspire and equip new church pastors to move beyond the fears associated with starting a new faith community and church turnarounds.

2. To inspire and equip congregations, who are seeking to start something new and create something different. To go forward with expected hope.

Introduction

Calling – "You can run but you can't hide!"

Since my early childhood years around the age of ten and eleven years old, I can recall a distinct feeling to know more and do more in the service of God. I wrestled with this silently because I felt this feeling was common for those who attended church regularly. Especially someone who had a parent who was a minister. But as I grew older I reluctantly began to pay more attention to this feeling, also hoping it was the spiritual effect of a young man who at a very young age knew more about the church than arguably any other subject.

As time progressed I journeyed through high school to college. It was also in college where the same type of labeling started. I did all I could to try to act differently but people could see right through me. During my sophomore year of college, I came home to sing in my home church choir anniversary. It was at that moment in front of church family and college friends that God exploded in my heart in such a dynamic way, that I have never been the same. Although people were certain at that point I would openly declare being called to the ministry, I was still content to hold out a little longer.

On February 19, 1992, at the age the age of twenty-two years old, I preached my initial trial sermon. It was clear in my heart and mind that I was following the will of God. This was not a start, but a continuation of what God had begun many years before. I had never felt more secure and sure of anything else in my life. A preacher of the Gospel is who I was going to be.

Through my personal journey and the church's journey, I discovered a biblical, God-given principle: We must Lose 2 Win! Come on the L2W journey with me....

CHAPTER 1

No Fear: Risking It All to Gain It All

*That is why, for Christ's sake,
I delight in weaknesses, in insults,
in hardships, in persecutions, in difficulties.
For when I am weak, then I am strong.*

(2 Corinthians 12:10)

The German philosopher, Fredrick Nietzche wrote, "That which does not kill us, makes us stronger." Today, quite a few quotes and song lyrics are floating around on the Internet that mimic this saying. While it does have some truth in it, I've never been fully convinced that the full truth is captured in Nietzche's words or the conventional wisdom retooling them.

Many popular myths shape our thinking. What's a myth? It's partially true for some people, some of the time, and in some situations. So, what seems true and truly real for one person may, in fact, work for others…or not.

As believers, we don't have to live our lives by trial and error—trying out conventional wisdom and popular myths. Instead, we can risk everything and go "all-in" all the time when we make right decision rooted in biblical truth. In contrast with popular myths, we can live life rooted in absolute truth—what's true for all people, all the time, and in all situations. The Truth himself, Jesus Christ, declares that God's truth is what set's us free: "If you hold to my teaching, you are really my disciples. Then you will know the truth, and the truth will set you free" (John 8:32).

I can vouch for the absolute truth reveal by Paul when he wrote to the Corinthians…

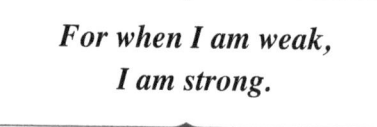

For when I am weak,
I am strong.

My Season of Hardship & Weakness

I became acquainted with this text in an intimate and personal way in 1994 when I was diagnosed with Hodgkin's disease. A mass the size of a small baseball was discovered by my doctors. The tumor was near my lungs. This diagnosis unexpectedly came out of nowhere. Believe me, I didn't want to hear it; it was unwelcomed news and my weakness became a huge disruption not only in my daily life but also in my future plans.

When I was going through a routine physical for my ministry ordination, this devastating diagnosis surfaced. What was both strange and interesting is that I had several physical exams in the my past when I was in the military and afterward through my personal physician. Those physicals pronounced me in good health. However, this was the first time that the tumor, or mass as it was called, was discovered.

My doctors assured me that after surgery and six months of extreme chemotherapy and radiation that the chances of my total recovery were very high. I would be cured. So, I thought that their recommendation was a small price to pay in order to live. But then they also informed me that the extreme treatments of chemotherapy could have an adverse effect on men causing infertility.

The risk I faced was losing the ability to be a biological father. I was also facing the pain and hardship of enduring drastic medical procedure that would make me sick in order to get better. Here's how I sum up the truth from this, I had to…

"Lose to win again."

No one made this statement to me then. However, looking back now with hindsight, I understand that I was making a decision to give up something, to risk being vulnerable in my body, to get rid of that which was unhealthy, in order to gain health on the other end, and yes…ultimately live.

Dr. Steve Maraboli says it this way, "Life sure can hit you hard! Suddenly, when you least expect it, WHAM; life has a knack for challenging you in ways that you don't feel prepared for. I feel like life sometimes tests and shapes you in a manner in which you feel least equipped. It seems you don't get to choose the exercise equipment the Universe challenges and builds your strength with."[1]

Overcoming a Victim Mindset

When something like this happens to you or me, it's tempting to adopt a victim mindset. It's easy to feel stuck, defeated, and like you are a losing player in the

---

[1] https://en.wikiquote.org/wiki/Steve_Maraboli

game of life. This victim mindset argues (very loudly) that you have lost; that nothing good is on the horizon.

Perhaps you have noticed the scientific theory/philosophy that often becomes a reality in life: *for every action, there's a reaction…for every cause, an effect…for every stimulus a response…and so on.* This is called the principle of causality or determinism:

> "All certainty in our relationships with the world rests on acknowledgment of causality. Causality is a genetic connection of phenomena through which one thing (the cause) under certain conditions gives rise to, causes something else (the effect). The essence of causality is the generation and determination of one phenomenon by another. In this respect, causality differs from various other kinds of connection, for example, the simple temporal sequence of phenomena, of the regularities of accompanying processes. For example, a pinprick causes pain. Brain damage causes mental illness. Causality is an active relationship, a relationship which brings to life something new, which turns possibility into actuality. A cause is an active and primary thing in relation to the effect."[2]

---

[2] https://www.marxists.org/reference/archive/spirkin/works/dialectical-materialism/ch02-s06.html

Now, determinism or the principle of cause and effect (causality) is a popular theory, or in my words, a myth — true for some people, some of the time, and in some situations. Such a myth can lead to a few crippling, irrational thoughts or myths, that develop a victim mindset within us. One renown psychologist, Albert Ellis (developed Rational Emotive Therapy), described a few of the irrational thoughts that victims carry around in their souls or psyches.

1. *I must do well and get the approval of everybody who matters to me or I will be a worthless person.*

2. *Other people must treat me kindly and fairly or else they are bad.*

3. *I must have an easy, enjoyable life or I cannot enjoy living at all.*

4. *All the people who matter to me must love me and approve of me or it will be awful.*

5. *I must be a high achiever, or I will be worthless.*

6. *Nobody should ever behave badly and if they do I should condemn them.*

7. *I mustn't be frustrated in getting what I want and if I am it will be terrible.*

8. *When things are tough, and I am under pressure I must be miserable and there is nothing I can do about this.*

9. *When faced with the possibility of something frightening or dangerous happening to me I must obsess about it and make frantic efforts to avoid it.*

10. *I can avoid my responsibilities and dealing with life's difficulties and still be fulfilled.*

11. *My past is the most important part of my life and it will keep on dictating how I feel and what I do.*

12. *Everybody and everything should be better than they are and, if they're not, it's awful.*

13. *I can be as happy as is possible by doing as little as I can and by just enjoying myself.*[3]

Do you notice the cause and effect nature of these statements? Look at number 11. A victim believes that one's past determines one's present and future. These

---

[3] http://www.padraigomorain.com/13-irrational-beliefs-albert-ellis.html

statements or irrational thoughts reveal that one's happiness is eternally controlled by others or events. In other words, victims believe that how they feel, think, and act is controlled by outside causes. They are victims—helpless to overcome life's problems, hardships, and difficulties.

Look over the list of victim beliefs. Which ones do you adhere to or even strongly believe? In my situation with a cancer diagnosis, I could have defaulted to a victim mindset and said, "Under these circumstances, I am destined to die. My genetics or toxic environment has doomed me. Cancer is in control of my life now and in the future. I am hopeless and helpless."

We are not "under our circumstances;" we are over them, i.e. overcomers! In Christ, we are not victims; we are victors. We can renew our minds from the way the myths of the world have programmed them and become more than conquerors through Christ. How does that happen? We can have a "lose to win" attitude that overcomes the world. Let's discover together how that happens.

Developing a "Lose to Win" Attitude

Never forget that the volume of an argument or the plausibility of a myth, theory, or popular notion does not reflect the validity or truth of that argument. Just because the victim mentality argues that we are losing, doesn't mean that it's true. In fact, I have come to realize that during the times in my life where I thought I was losing, I was actually winning. I have discovered that:

"Some of the greatest messages come out of the greatest messes."

I also believe that no matter how big the mess, problem, issue or challenge, it doesn't hinder God's ability to bless and make us stronger. I've learned that sometimes we have to back up in order to go forward. John Maxwell calls it "failing forward."

- *You have to give a little to get more.*
- *You must step aside in order to step up.*

Dr. Maroboli writes, "It is when I struggled that I found my strength. It is when challenged to my core that I learn the depth of who I am. It is when we feel broken that we can become experts at mending."[4] Paul's "lose to win" mindset prompts this response in him: *I delight in weaknesses, in insults, in hardships, in persecutions, in difficulties.* At the end of his life when imprisoned in

---

[4] Steve Maraboli - A Better Today - 2013

Rome, he writes to the Philippians, "Rejoice in the Lord always. I will say it again: Rejoice! ...I have learned to be content whatever the circumstances. I know what it is to be in need, and I know what it is to have plenty. I have learned the secret of being content in any and every situation, whether well fed or hungry, whether living in plenty or in want. I can do everything through him who gives me strength" (Philippians 4:4, 11b-13).

With a cause-and-effect mindset, how would a victim/loser respond to Paul's list of "bad" or "negative" situations and experiences?

- Weaknesses [Greek: *astheneia*] disease, infirmity, sickness, feebleness, malady.
- Insults [Greek: *hubris*] injury, harm, insult, reproach.
- Hardships [Greek: *anagke*] distress, being needy, lacking the necessities of life.
- Persecutions [Greek: *diogmos*] molestation, harassment, abuse, maltreatment.
- Difficulties [Greek: *stenochooias*] extreme affliction, dire calamity.

I dare say a victim's mindset would respond with extreme, negative emotions like depression, anxiety, worry, despair, dejection, hurt, and anger, to name a few. Yet Paul's "lose to win" attitude is summed up with the word, "delight." Let's unpack that attitude: (Greek for "delight" is *eudokeoo*.]

- *To take pleasure in or be happy.*
- *To seem good to one.*
- *To take satisfaction in.*
- *To see as a benefit.*
- *To rejoice in.*

When we "lose to win," we are predisposed, that is, we have chosen before the fact to respond to a situation like cancer with an attitude like:

I am not fearful. I will risk pain and weakness to gain strength and health.

When I chose a lose-to-win attitude, I discovered a journey that responded to God's truth and good plans for my life instead of caving into fear, doubt, and desperation.

My "Lose to Win" Journey

My journey out of cancer and weakness, into health and strength, has taken me into ministry and planting a church named Journey. I've been reflecting on the

Journey story, as I am writing this book and we approach our twelve-year "journeyversary." God has given us a theme of "All In" meaning we are invested, involved, and inviting. But I can still remember, the shock and amazement and wonder of many of my friends, colleagues, and family when they learned I was planning to start a new church.

After eleven years of pastoring in Spartanburg, in 2006 I took a conference staff position coaching churches. I then chose to plant a church. My father asked me, "Are you going to leave that conference job to start a new church with no members?"

I remember my youngest son asking my wife, after one of our initial taste and see services in 2007, momma did daddy make the Bishop mad, where's our church? There are times when you must be willing to risk it all in order to gain it all. All in for Christ.

In our text Paul finds himself in this great paradox of life, losing to win. Paul writes,

To keep me from becoming conceited because of these surpassingly great revelations, there was given me a thorn in my flesh, a messenger of Satan, to torment me. Three times I pleaded with the Lord to take it away from me. But he said to me, "My grace is sufficient for you, for my power is made perfect in weakness." Therefore I will boast all the more gladly about my weaknesses, so that Christ's power may rest on me. That is why, for Christ's sake, I delight in weaknesses, in insults, in hardships, in persecutions, in difficulties. For when I am weak, then I am strong. (2 Corinthians 7-10)

At the beginning of the text, Paul addresses a personal problem. He invites us in to witness how he wrestles with his ordeal. When faced with the ordeal of a thorn in his flesh, Paul uses the spiritual discipline of prayer to plead his case before the Lord. Three times the text tells us he went to God. I believe the significance is in his persistence to seek God in what could be perceived as a losing situation. How do we overcome the temptation to embrace a victim mindset?

Persist in Prayer.

Listen for God's Lesson.

Accept His "Lose to Win" Attitude.

Wait a minute, you may chide. You came up with that catchphrase, "Lose to Win." No, God gave me that lesson and phrase when I needed to overcome cancer's attack on me. Quite frankly, the lessons of the Incarnation and the Cross, as well as our being, conform to Christ's image, are all "lose to win" lessons. Philippians 2 tells us how Jesus left His exalted place in glory, became a human being and a servant, humbled himself, and died on the cross. As Bill Hybels writes, that was descending into greatness—lose glory to win over death. When we are conformed to his image, we lose or sacrifice ourselves, die to our ego and pride, are buried in the waters of repentance and baptism in order to be raised up with His indwelling Spirit and image in us (Read Galatians 2 and Romans 6, 12).

The whole of the Christian walk in following Jesus Christ is to take up our cross and follow Him. That's *lose to win*. We lose nothing of value and gain everything through His mercy and grace.

God's lesson for Paul was that His abundant grace is sufficient to cover Paul's meager loss.

It's not what we go through but how we go through it that makes a difference. Instead of reacting as victims, we can choose to respond as more than conquerors through Christ who loves us.

- Trusting and depending on God's grace kept me in the right frame of mind.

- Trusting and depending on God's grace allowed me to get a glimpse of God's redemption that was taking me through losing to winning.
- Trusting in God's grace gave me peace to handle the outcome no matter what.

I had to *Persist in Prayer* to *Listen for God's Lesson* in order to develop God's *Lose to Win* mindset in overcoming not just cancer, but also my fears, negative emotions, and worthless efforts to pull myself up by my own pride and self-centeredness. I learned the lesson that the real issues and problems we encounter in life's journey are not external but rather internal. The journey's battles are won not in time and space but in our souls and spirits.

**God revealed that my greatest affliction was compatible
with my greatest strength—my relationship with Christ.
In my weakness, He was strong.
His grace was sufficient to lift me up
from my deepest valley.**

Paul said, *Therefore I am content with or delight in (rejoice in) hardships, calamities, insults, etc.*

We are all affected by the storms and struggles of life. How are we to respond? Trapped within the myth of causality or liberated by the truth of grace. Consider a tennis ball or play dough? When we put pressure on play dough, it leaves a lasting imprint. Everybody sees the marks that are left.

However, if we put pressure on a tennis ball, although it does cave in, it doesn't remain in that condition. IT always bounces back to its original shape.

How do we respond to the pressures and struggles of life? Like the tennis ball or like the play dough. Caving in or bouncing back. It's a matter of what you're made of! Our struggles either make us bitter or better.

Out of the hard times, good can come.

Lose to win again.

Are you willing to risk it all…

to gain it all?

Persist in Prayer...

Write a prayer that asks God how you are to respond to your present problem, pressure, or pain?

_____

_____

_____

_____

_____

_____

_____

_____

_____

_____

_____

_____

_____

Listen for God's Lesson…

Write down the truth in the Scriptures that He speaks to you:

God's *Lose to Win* Attitude…

What is the attitude for overcoming that God is asking you to declare and act upon:

_____

_____

_____

_____

_____

_____

_____

_____

_____

_____

_____

_____

Put Yourself into the Scripture

At the end of each chapter, I will invite you to take a scripture passage used in the chapter and put your name into each blank, read the text out loud throughout a day or a week until it is engraved on your heart, etched in your mind, and embossed in your spirit. From The Message, here is an adaption of 2 Corinthians 12:9-10…

God told _____,
My grace is enough; it's all _____ needs.
My strength comes into its own in
_____'s weakness.
Once I heard that _____ was glad to let it happen.
_____ quit focusing on the handicap and began
appreciating the gift.
It was a case of Christ's strength moving in on
_____'s weakness.
Now _____ takes limitations in stride, and with good cheer, these limitations that cut _____
down to size—abuse, accidents, opposition,
bad breaks.
_____, just let Christ take over!
And so the weaker _____ gets,
the stronger _____ becomes.

CHAPTER 2

Make Defeat Your Fuel

Because of the extravagance of those revelations, and so I wouldn't get a big head, I was given the gift of a handicap to keep me in constant touch with my limitations. Satan's angel did his best to get me down; what he in fact did was push me to my knees. No danger then of walking around high and mighty! At first, I didn't think of it as a gift and begged God to remove it. Three times I did that, and then he told me,

My grace is enough; it's all you need.

My strength comes into its own in your weakness. Once I heard that I was glad to let it happen. I quit focusing on the handicap and began appreciating the gift. It was a case of Christ's strength moving in on my weakness. Now I take limitations in stride, and with good cheer, these limitations that cut me down to size—abuse, accidents, opposition, bad breaks. I just let Christ take over! And so the weaker I get, the stronger I become.

(2 Corinthians 12:7-10 MSG)

I am who I am today because the tears of my past have watered the flowers of my present. I'm stronger because I've learned the blessing of pressing through difficulties and disappointment.

In the midst of struggles and pain, I've learned to find strength. Struggle for a Christian, for a child of God, does not mean that God is not there. Nor is the trial a means of punishment or judgment because you are doing something wrong. In many instances, it's to be expected.

Physical Pain Producing Superhuman Strength

Ever talk with someone who has been through rehab after a back or knee surgery. They often weep when they recount the excruciating pain of the exercises the physical therapist puts them through as they slowly and systematically build up their strength.

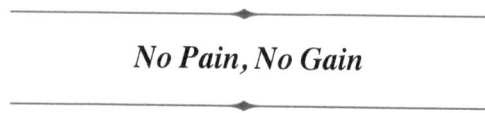

No Pain, No Gain

Jane Fonda first made this statement currently popular in her workout videos…she would shout this out and then say, "Feel the burn." Surely, you have heard this physical exercise motto from coaches, trainers, and even doctors.

The beneficial type of pain from exercise happens when microscopic muscle fibers actually tear and then they rebuild becoming a denser, stronger muscle. Remember the biblical story about Israel's judge, Samson. He is weakened by breaking his Nazarite vow to not cut his hair; he allowed Delilah to cut his hear and thus lost his God-given strength. After being imprisoned by the Philistines and being required to daily turn a heavy stone grinder of grain. As he pushed the grinding wheel day after day, his hair grew, and his strength grew through the pain. Then one day, the Philistines decided to mock him in their temple of Dagon. They had him brought to a pagan celebration, but as he stood between two pillars of that temple, he wrapped his arms around them, pushed, and brought down the roof upon himself and the whole crowd was destroyed.

Samson's physical as well as spiritual pain served to strengthen him and bring him back to God as well as overcome his enemies. God allows us to experience trials and tribulations. In the process, we develop strength—body, soul, and spirit. Consider St. Paul's description of this process of gain through pain:

> *Therefore, having been justified by faith, we have peace with God through our Lord Jesus Christ, through whom also we have access by faith into this grace in which we stand, and*

rejoice in hope of the glory of God. And not only that, but we also glory in tribulations, knowing that tribulation produces perseverance; and perseverance, character; and character, hope. Now hope does not disappoint, because the love of God has been poured out in our hearts by the Holy Spirit who was given to us. (Romans 5:1-5)

Earlier I shared with you my bout with physical disease and how through the struggle, I gained physical, emotional, and spiritual strength. We must lose to win. We lose our own, natural strength; yet, in our weakness, Christ becomes our strength.

When trials and tribulations come upon us—a financial crisis, a painful hurt in a relationship, a physical ailment, a job loss, demotion or probation, how do we respond? In his book, *Respond Up!*, Don Newman writes about the choice we have when situations, problems, and issues arise in our lives:

> *The way you move forward in life is greatly dictated by how you respond to life.*

- *Life happens, and we can either "react" or learn to "respond."*

- *Choosing to respond instead of reacting out of our past patterns not only leads us forward but can also be the key to promotion.*

- *There is a big difference between choosing to become a "first-responder" and just being a "first-reactor."*

- *The real power to become a person who responds instead of reacts comes from where your response begins...respond up!*[5]

My first question for you, is, "Do you respond up or react down when life's trials come your way?" So, here's is God's process of growth for you and me when trials come our way.

Don't just go through difficulties, grow through them.

Growing Through Not Around Life's Tests

Psalm 23 tells us that we go through the valleys. Psalm 34:19 (ESV) assures us, "Many are the afflictions of the righteous, but the Lord delivers him out of them

---

[5] Newman, Don. *Respond Up!* Maitland, FL: 302 Books, 2018, p. xi-xii

all." Psalm 119:71 teaches us, "It was good for me to be afflicted so that I might learn your decrees."

We need to "Lose To Win!" What are we losing? We lose our impatience, our *I want to quit* attitude, our "pity party" mindset, and our "If I don't get my way, I want no way" selfishness. And what do we win according to Romans 5? We win "perseverance." Let me unpack that for you. The Greek word translated *perseverance* in this verse is *hypomone* which means "patience, waiting on the Lord with hopeful expectation, enduring trials until good fruit is produced."

Too often, our difficulties bear the fruit in our lives of impatience and complaining. What about you. Are you responding up or reacting down, joyfully or sadly, impatiently or waiting hopefully? Life is filled with choices. We cannot always control what happens in our lives, but we can responsibly respond by choosing *perseverance*.

Then Paul writes that "perseverance produces character." Two words are used here that we can learn from *produces/worketh* and *character/experience*. The fire of suffering can burn us up or refine us as gold and produce diamonds in life instead of coal. Our experiences in life can shape our character with integrity and courage or work discouragement and disillusionment within us. If godly character emerges through our life's trials, then hope grows within us as a fruit of God's Spirit. I know everyone loves Jeremiah 29:11 "For I know the plans I have for you," declares the LORD, "plans to prosper you and not to harm you, plans to give you hope and a future." But what comes in Jeremiah before Jeremiah 29:11? But before we run off with Jeremiah 29:11, we must realize the other twenty-eight chapters that come before the twenty-ninth. Jeremiah said in chapter 8:18-22,

> *My joy is gone, grief is upon me, my heart is sick. Hark, the cry of my poor people from far and wide in the land: "Is the Lord not in Zion? Is her King not in her?" ("Why have they provoked me to anger with their images, with their foreign idols?") "The harvest is past, the summer is ended, and we are not saved." For the hurt of my poor people I am hurt, I mourn, and dismay has taken hold of me. Is there no balm in Gilead? Is there no physician there? Why then has the health of my poor people not been restored?"*

The experience that Jeremiah had before he wrote chapter 29 produced grief, loss, and pain. But he went through all of that to win hope and celebrate the goodness of God's plans for his life and for Israel. **Lose to Win!**

My grandmother Pearl was strong-willed Christian woman. She and my grandfather owned a farm and raised ten children. Grandma Pearl was a remarkable homemaker and artisan. She made gorgeous quilts, clothes, and doll dresses. She was a excellent cook and baker. All of this was made all the more remarkable by the fact that she only had one arm.

One day right after she gave birth to her first son, she was outside tending to the barrel where trash was burned and while outside she became dizzy and fell partially into the barrel. The side of his face was burned and her sleeve where she cradled him caught fire. Her arm was burned severely, and not being able to see a doctor immediately eventually her arm needed to be amputated.

The grandmother I remember had no limitations, even as she endured having a double mastectomy. Her body weekend, but her spirit was strong. Each day that she spent with me and my sisters as she sat with us after we would get out of school, she exemplified strength. She would she have us sing a song, "Do you know the man, do you know the man, do you know the man from Galilee he walked out on the water and calmed the raging sea, do you know the man from Galilee." Grandma Pearl made defeat her fuel.

Put Yourself into the Scripture

Take this scripture passage and put your name into each blank, read the text out loud throughout a day or a week until it is engraved on your heart, etched in your mind, and embossed in your spirit. After Paul wrote this,

"Five times I received from the Jews the forty lashes minus one. Three times I was beaten with rods, once I was pelted with stones, three times I was shipwrecked, I spent a night and a day in the open sea, I have been constantly on the move. I have been in danger from rivers, in danger from bandits, in danger from my fellow Jews, in danger from Gentiles; in danger in the city, in danger in the country, in danger at sea; and in danger from false believers. I have labored and toiled and have often gone without sleep; I have known hunger and thirst and have often gone without food; I have been cold and naked. Besides everything else, I face daily the pressure of my concern for all the churches." (2 Cor 11:24-28)

Paul responded with this and so can you:

"God is at work in all things for the good of _____ who loves Him and is called according to His purpose." (Romans 8:28)

What challenges are you facing today that can be strengthening you for tomorrow?

When was a time when you won because you lost?

Who are the toxic people you need to release from your focus in order to win the peace of God that can come to you through godly relationships?

CHAPTER 3

Your Best Life

*Then he said to them all,
"If any want to become my followers,
let them deny themselves
and take up their cross daily and follow me.
For those who want to save their life will lose it,
and those who lose their life for my sake will save it.*

(Luke 9:23-24)

I am admittedly one of those people who never likes to lose. In fact, I must confess that at time I have been known as a sore loser. A sore loser is someone who loses in a fair competition but whines about it on a constant basis, blaming everyone else for their loss except themselves. Such a sore loser may be fun to taunt but is certainly no fun to play with.

As a sports enthusiast, I was always intrigued at the end of a game be football, basketball, baseball or boxing to watch and see how the losing team would go over and shake the hands of the players of the winning team. For example, if you are a boxer and your opponent has just finished whipping up on you, after the fight, you must go over, shake hands, and say: *Good match*.

I remember watching the Cleveland Cavaliers, Lebron aka King James, Kiaree, Kevin Love in game five of the NBA championship finals lose to Steph Curry, Kevin Durant, and the Golden State Warriors. I watched King James and the boys go over and shake their opponents' hands in defeat and say. *Good Game*. Although I know it's the right thing to do, I must admit it's very hard to lose with dignity and respect. I asked some former athletes about this and remember one of them saying, "Rev, it's not that the losing doesn't hurt, because it does hurt, but my focus is on the next time we play, I plan to win." Now that's a lose-to-win attitude.

What Are You Hanging On To?

Luke 9:24 in the New Living Translation reads,

If you try to hang on to your life, you will lose it. But if you give up your life for my sake, you will save it."

Permit me to unpack for a moment this phrase, *if you try to hang on to your life, you will lose it*. What adjectives can we use to describe what we humans hang onto in life that makes us "lose it," i.e. lose our zest for living life to the full? Hanging onto the old life, the past, filled with loses, failures, hurts, pain, sin, regrets, and trauma really creates what psychologists now call Post Traumatic Stress Syndrome. Living in the past fills today and tomorrow with PTSD.

Are you hanging onto *drama and trauma?* You may say to me, "I thought PTSD was an illness reserved for war veterans." Really? Life is a battle, a war if you will. Every game in sports is a battle…a war against the opponents, the other team or player. We fight on the job, with family members or even church members. We battle with finances, bill and debt collectors, and those pundits we disagree with in politics and government. Facebook, Twitter, and social media, in general, is filled with acrimony, disagreements, verbal jabs, put-downs, and hateful taunts. Bullying has become a crisis in our schools. Life has become a battlefield filled with abuse, prejudice, and anger—all of which create trauma and stress. When we hang onto our past, the old life filled with loses and failures, then we continually experience PTSD.

Post means "after the fact." Once something is over, in the past, the only way it can come to life is if you give it energy, memory, regret, or worry. I have an intriguing acronym for worry. "W" stands for *waste* – worry wastes your time, energy, and resources in the present. "O" stands for *obsession, thinking about past traumas over and over again*. In other words, worry causes you to obsess about your past—to go over and over again your mistakes, failures, and trauma. The two r's in worry are regression and regret. Instead of growing, maturing and making progress we regress into childish beliefs and fears. We dwell with regrets constantly plummeting ourselves with the bludgeons of "what if" or "if only." Finally, the "Y" simply means *yesterday*. For those who worry, who exist in the purgatory of "after the fact," there are no new today's or hopeful tomorrows, only traumatic, stressful yesterdays.

Jesus recognized the reality of the PTSD we face in living life. He said things like…

> *Do not worry about tomorrow,*
> *for tomorrow will worry about its own things.*
> *Sufficient for the day is its own trouble*
> (Matthew 6:34).

In the world, you will have tribulation [trials, sufferings], But be of good cheer, I have overcome the world (John 16:33).

In order to live a new life in Christ without PTSD, we must die to the old life. Tired of the fight? Worn out trying to hang onto the past? God has powerful, freeing, life-renewing advice for you. Consider taking His prescription in Isaiah 43:18-19. Read His words from two different perspectives or translations:

> "Forget about what's happened;
> don't keep going over old history.
> Be alert, be present. I'm about to do something brand-new.
> It's bursting out! Don't you see it?
> There it is! I'm making a road through the desert, rivers in the badlands." (*The Message*)

> "Forget the former things;
> do not dwell on the past. See, I am doing a new thing!
> Now it springs up; do you not perceive it?
> I am making a way in the desert
> and streams in the wasteland." (*NIV*)

In order to live our best life, we cannot hang onto our old life—the past with all its worries, sorrows, pain and guilt. The old life is a desert, a wasteland. So, Jesus says, *Die to it*. I have a counselor friend whose office wall behind his desk has this sign on it:

Get Over It!

What worry, what PTSD are you hanging onto? What deadly memory from the past do you keep obsessing over? What trauma is robbing you of your joy? A divorce. Bankruptcy. Foreclosure. Rejection. Lost position or job. Broken relationship with a parent or child? A failure business? An unfulfilled expectation of yourself or another person? A broken promise or a broken heart?

Hear again God's prescription which isn't an opiate to dull the pain; His words are life to replace the death caused by pain: *Forget the former things; do not dwell on the past. See, I am doing a new thing!* As long as you drive through life looking in a rearview mirror, you will crash.

When you are someone you know says, *My life's a wreck*, now you have a response. You have a choice. Hang out at the crash scene or get over it, move beyond it, die to yourself to live anew in God's future for you. He is making a way out of your desert and into something brand-new.

Living Your Best Life

What happens when your Best Life is tied to you moving forward and leaving the past behind, i.e. losing to win? It's like...

- *losing weight or getting in shape and gaining better health.*
- *losing that addiction to spending you gain financial freedom from debt.*
- *losing that addiction to hanging on to toxic people in your life you gain peace of mind.*
- *losing your PTSD and winning back your sanity.*

When you die to that old person you were, you finally get rid of that person driving you crazy all the time filling your head with mess! The old "you" is filled with irrational beliefs, toxic feelings, and destructive behaviors. To live your best life, you must release, let go of, and get over the negative past.

Irrational Beliefs. Psychologist Albert Ellis identified the irrational beliefs that trap us in our past and literally make us crazy:

- It is a dire necessity for adult humans to be loved or approved by virtually every significant other person in their community.

- One absolutely must be competent, adequate and achieving in all important respects or else one is an inadequate, worthless person.
- People absolutely must act considerately and fairly, and they are damnable villains if they do not. They *are* their bad acts.
- It is awful and terrible when things are not the way one would very much like them to be.
- Emotional disturbance is mainly externally caused, and people have little or no ability to increase or decrease their dysfunctional feelings and behaviors.
- If something is or may be dangerous or fearsome, then one should be constantly and excessively concerned about it and should keep dwelling on the possibility of it occurring.
- One cannot and must not face life's responsibilities and difficulties and it is easier to avoid them.
- One must be quite dependent on others and need them and you cannot mainly run one's own life.
- One's past history is an all-important determiner of one's present behavior and because something once strongly affected one's life, it should indefinitely have a similar effect.
- Other people's disturbances are horrible, and one must feel upset about them.

- There is invariably a right, precise and perfect solution to human problems and it is awful if this perfect solution is not found.[6]

Take a moment. Any of the above beliefs do you sometimes or always have, then circle that statement. Anything you circle is the old you and you must die to it. Will you release it…let it go? Will you embrace the fact that God loves you and has created you to be a loveable and capable, wonderfully made person? Will you start singing that beautiful children's song, "I am lovable and capable"? Bury the old, irrational thoughts and think this way to live your best life:

> "Summing it all up, friends, I'd say you'll do best by filling your minds and meditating on things true, noble, reputable, authentic, compelling, gracious — the best, not the worst; the beautiful, not the ugly; things to praise, not things to curse. Put into practice what you learned from me, what you heard and saw and realized. Do that, and God, who makes everything work together, will work you into his most excellent harmonies." (Philippians 4:8-10 MSG)

Toxic Feelings. You will never live your best life until you feel the best. Toxic feeling…negative feelings…

---

[6] http://changingminds.org/explanations/belief/irrational_beliefs.htm

drain you of faith, hope, and love. Feelings like anger, hate, worry, revenge, spite, fear, doubt, jealousy, depression, despair, oh you know all too well where this list is headed. My prayer is that you will choose to bury your toxic feelings…die to them. Let God's Spirit sow the seeds of Christ's character into you so that you will bear the fruit of love, joy, peace, patience, kindness, goodness and self-control (Galatians 5:22).

Destructive Behaviors. What habitual words or actions do you have that hurt others or yourself? God's love in you conquers all and covers over a multitude of sin. Every thought, feeling, and action is a choice, not a chain. You are not bound by past irrational thoughts, toxic feelings, or destructive behaviors. Christ has set you free to love God, others and yourself. That freedom starts with losing your old life and receiving God's new life for you.

Start Living Your Best Life NOW!

Losing the old can wake you up and see life from a different perspective. In our text, Jesus makes it clear that true fulfillment, your best life is achieved in pursuit of His will ruling our own lives. As we do live in God's newness, we discover that He has rescued us from our past while making us secure in Him…now and forever. "For those who want to save their life will lose it, and those who lose their life for my sake will save it…Therefore I am content with weaknesses, insults, hardships, persecutions, and calamities for the sake of Christ; for whenever I am weak, then I am strong" (Luke 9:23-24; 2 Corinthians 12:10 MSG).

Does that mean that your best life is free of trials, tribulation, and trauma? In the Message Bible, we read Jesus saying, "It is necessary that the Son of Man proceed to an ordeal of suffering, be tried and found guilty by the religious leaders, high priests, and religion scholars, be killed, and on the third day be raised up alive" (Luke 9:21). Then Jesus told us what to expect: "Anyone who intends to come with me has to let me lead. You're not in the driver's seat—I am. Don't run from suffering; embrace it. Follow me and I'll show you how. Self-help is no help at all. Self-sacrifice is the way, my way, to finding yourself, your true self. What kind of deal is it to get everything you want but lose yourself? What could you ever trade your soul for?" (Luke 9:21-23 MSG)

Lose to win your best life. Will your best life involve a fight filled with battles? Of course. After all the battles, what will be the outcome of your best life? Paul describes your future when you will be able to say as he did:

I have fought the good fight.
I have finished the race.
I have kept the faith.

(2 Timothy 4:7)

Out with the old you; in with the new. Trust God to bring out your best. "Unlike the culture around you, always dragging you down to its level of maturity, God brings out the best in you, develops well-formed maturity in you."[7] Losing to win with God in control of you…

Now that's the best life ever!

Put Yourself into the Scripture

Take this scripture passage and put your name into each blank, read the text out loud throughout a day or a week until it is engraved on your heart, etched in your mind, and embossed in your spirit. Jesus is saying to you…

"_____ who intends to come with me has to let me lead. _____ is not in the driver's seat—I am. Don't run from suffering; embrace it. _____, follow me and I'll show you how. Self-help is no help at all. Self-sacrifice is the way, my way, to finding yourself, your true self. What kind of deal is it to get everything _____ wants

---

[7] Romans 12:2 MSG

but lose yourself? What could _____ ever trade your soul for?" (Luke 9:21-23 MSG)

So, make a list of the worries from the past you have been hanging onto which you will know release and let die:

_____

_____

_____

_____

_____

_____

_____

_____

_____

_____

_____

CHAPTER 4

God's Big Payback

This is what GOD says, the God who builds a road right through the ocean, who carves a path through pounding waves, The God who summons horses and chariots and armies— they lie down and then can't get up; they're snuffed out like so many candles: "*Forget about what's happened;*

> *don't keep going over old history.*
> *Be alert, be present.*
> *I'm about to do something brand-new.*
> *It's bursting out! Don't you see it?*
> *There it is! I'm making a road through the desert, rivers in the badlands."*

Wild animals will say 'Thank you!' —the coyotes and the buzzards—
Because I provided water in the desert,

rivers through the sun-baked earth,
Drinking water for the people I chose,
the people I made especially for myself,
a people custom-made to praise me.

(Isaiah 43:16-21) Message Bible

As you study the history of Israel, you will find out that God always made a way for them through bondage, slavery, and suffering to freedom. He made a way to get them out of Egypt, He made a way for them to cross the Red Sea, He made a way for them in the crossing of the wilderness, and He made a way for them to go into the Promised Land.

When you follow God, He will make a way…

Through your bondage to your release.
Through your illness to your healing.
Through your disappointment to His promises for you.
Through your grief to your joy.
Through your self-centeredness to your calling to love others.
Through your sin to your redemptions.

The second portion of Isaiah beginning with chapter forty and thus chapters forty-three and beyond, reveals how God will make Jerusalem the center of his worldwide rule through a royal savior, the Messiah or Anointed One, who will destroy her enemies.

God reminded Israel that "I am the God who brings you out and brings you through trouble." You might say, "Preacher, I don't have any trouble." Well, put this promise from God in your hip pocket because you will need it later. In John 16:33 Jesus said, "I have told you these things, so that in me you may have peace. In this world you will have trouble. But take heart! I have overcome the world."

What I Want vs. What I Need

Some of us hope for a stress-free, trouble-free and pain-free life. Ever spent time walking down the Walmart pharmacy aisle surveying all the pain-relief medications. You've got your Ibuprofen like Advil and Motrin, your aspirins, your Acetaminophens like Tylenol, and your Naproxen like Alieve. They work for a while but cannot give lasting relief.

I've noticed that what people want is relief from their troubles, pain, and difficulties. God tells us that what we need is repentance—a complete change of direction and dependency. When we are going our own way, it's impossible to find God's way through our valleys.

When we are depending on the world's ways including drugs, pleasure and numbing ourselves with media, music, sports, games, and distractions we find ourselves in Egyptian slavery or Babylonian exile.

Follow the world's ways; get temporary relief. Follow God's way through your troubles; find lasting hope and healing. That requires repentance which is turning away from what we want and turning to what we need. Christ invites us to take up our cross (on which we crucify self and sin) and follow Him. The Promised Land is this:

> *And my God will meet all your needs*
> *according to his glorious riches in Christ Jesus.*
>
> (Philippians 4:19)

The Big Payback

Remember the words of Isaiah 40:1-7, how God displays his redemptive hand:

> Comfort, O comfort my people, says your God.
>
> ² Speak tenderly to Jerusalem, and cry to her that she has served her term, (THE BIG PAYBACK) that her penalty is paid, that she has received from the LORD's hand double for all her sins.

> ³A voice cries out: "In the wilderness prepare the way of the Lord, make straight in the desert a highway for our God. ⁴Every valley shall be lifted up, and every mountain and hill be made low; the uneven ground shall become level, and the rough places a plain.
>
> ⁵Then the glory of the Lord shall be revealed, and all people shall see it together, for the mouth of the Lord has spoken."
>
> ⁶A voice says, "Cry out!" And I said, "What shall I cry?" All people are grass, their constancy is like the flower of the field.
>
> ⁷The grass withers, the flower fades, when the breath of the Lord blows upon it; surely the people are grass.

There is only one source of lasting and eternal redemption in our lives. That source isn't our job, family, or the lottery. Yes, there's a television show that helps lottery winners spend their winnings on a dream home. Sadly, most lottery winners are poor again after a short time. Winning the lottery like all other worldly promises is a short-term payback. Our pensions, savings and 401k funds will not be a lasting source for boomers who hope to retire. FHA has even developed reverse mortgages to have the equity in our homes pay us back in old age. The truth is that the only lasting source or god who can redeem us and pay us back is the God of Abraham, Isaac, and Jacob. Isaiah 44:6 declares, "Thus says the Lord, the King of Israel and his Redeemer, the Lord of host; I am the first and I am the last, besides me there is no god.

Just as the Living God made an exodus for Israel out of Egypt and the Exile, He has made a way for us. In our church aptly named Journey, we've been on this church-planting journey for more than eight years from the warehouse years to the present worship center.

At the end of this book, I write about the ups and downs of the church planting journey. We journeyed from an abandoned, dusty, industrial building, which was cold in the winter and hot in the summer to the Clemson years, two years, as an infant church. We declared God as our source—not a building campaign, nor a denomination or a rich benefactor. Our chant was "Yes We Can," knowing that we could do all things through Christ who strengthens us.

But the Journey didn't stop there in the Clemson location; we outgrew that location, attempted to buy it, but God said keep moving. Our church, Journey, went back to school. We met in Longleaf Middle School, God's three-year plan, one for the Father, one for the Son and one for the Holy Ghost. We reached five hundred in worship with the theme "Mission Possible." Then, God was getting ready to do just what He promised He would do.

But the Journey didn't stop there, Christmas Sunday 2013, God gave us some keys to our own building for two worship services, one thousand members, babies, children, youth, adults ages 0-90 years old.

Will God Meet My Need? **You Ask...**

As you read this book, I'm sure you want to know: "When I'm in need can God make a way, Is God able? When my back is up against the wall when all hope is gone, will there be a path through the sea of grief, pain, loss, or despair that I face?

I can answer today in the affirmative: ***YES, GOD IS ABLE!***

If God was able to speak and the worlds began to twirl and spin on its axis;

If God was able to place the stars and planets in exact order around the sun;

If God was able to fashion man in His own image;

If God was able to take a rib and make a woman;

If God was able to number the hairs on every head that ever walked the face of the earth since time began;

If God was able to walk on water and say, "Peace, be still"

Then God is able to turn your sorrow in the night to joy in the morning.

No longer is your question, "Is God able to make a way through?"

Rather, ask yourself, "Am I willing and ready to follow Him wherever He leads."

Are you ready for a reversal of fortune, or a renewing of your mind, for a revival for your soul?

Isaiah 40:30-31 declares for each person following God:

> *Even youths will faint and be weary, and the young will fall exhausted; but those who wait for the Lord shall renew their strength, they shall mount up with wings like eagles, they shall run and not be weary, they shall walk and not faint.*

Tired of being down?

Tired of being the tale and not the head?

Tired of being broke busted and disgusted?

Tired of crying and weeping, grieving and dying on the inside?

It's time to get ready to follow the Way through, to follow Christ!

Are you ready?

Tell the Lord, "I'm ready."

"I'm watching the phone."

"I'm looking at the clock."

"I got my best clothes on."

"I'm standing at the door waiting for opportunity to knock."

"I've opened the door to my heart and put out the welcome sign."

The story is told of an only survivor of a wreck who was thrown on an uninhabited island. After a while, he managed to build himself a hut, in which he placed the little that he had saved from the wreck. He prayed to God for deliverance, and anxiously scanned the horizon each day to hail any passing ship.

One day on returning from a hunt for food he was horrified to find his hut in flames—all he had went up in smoke. The worst had happened it seemed. But that which seemed to have happened for the worst was in reality for the best. The next day a ship arrived. "We saw your smoke signal," the captain said.

The children of Israel stood on the Red Sea's bank and looked back. They saw death and destruction rampaging toward them—they were hopeless and without a way through. God parted the sea, they followed Him through, and their enemies were drowned and utterly destroyed.

Stop looking back…where you've been doesn't determine where you're going. Your impending destruction isn't your destiny. God is making a way through for you—trust and obey.

APPENDIX 1
NO FEAR

"old ways will not open new doors"

In establishing Journey Church in 2007, there were several questions that I wrestled with.

- Who was going to come?
- Would we have enough money?
- What if the church didn't grow?
- What if the church grew?
- What if we faced resistance from other churches?

In the gospel of Luke, the disciples went fishing one day and came back with nothing. They were discouraged. Jesus instructed them to cast their nets into the deep waters for a greater catch.

After years and years of catching nothing, declining numbers, frustrations, and disappointments, it seems that still today, many churches and pastors are dealing with the same issues the disciples faced. Christ message to the church parallels his message to the disciples. Choose some new options, change your strategy, and go in different direction. Go deeper!

What if everything you trusted and believed in changed? What if the path to the future demands a different course? What if your methods, systems, routines, processes are being challenged?

This my friends, is where I stood twenty five years ago when I started in ministry. In reality, I still stand there to this day. What has changed? I've dared to do things different. I've dared to go beyond the familiar. I've dared to lead, allowing faith to overcome my fears. I've dared to believe in a God size dream for my life and the church.

Our team recognized in order to be effective at reaching new people, we would have to embrace new ways of being the church within the community. Change would have to be embraced. Although we all loved and valued the ministry and the legacy of the past, there was a greater recognition and desire to move beyond what was familiar.

Isaiah 41:8-10 *"But you, Israel, are my servant. You're Jacob, my first choice, descendants of my good friend Abraham. I pulled you in from all over the world, called you in from every dark corner of the earth,*
Telling you, 'You're my servant, serving on my side. I've picked you. I haven't dropped you.' Don't panic. I'm with you. There's no need to fear for I'm your God.

I'll give you strength. I'll help you. I'll hold you steady, keep a firm grip on you." The Message Bible

Church Planting and Growth
Issues & Answers

Many pastors and church leaders desire to grow personally and grow their churches spiritually with the overall goal of numerical growth. Personal travail in many aspects will emerge during this process. Much of what is in this book is a spiritual journey of my personal travail, along with the church's spiritual growth. The purpose of this book is to provide churches with the tools and perspectives needed to further equip their members and leaders with a growth mindset.

Mature Christians involved in a church plant or considering joining a new church must remember that a growth mindset is critical to transitioning from an existing church to a church plant, or resurrecting a church from stagnation.

Recently, I was interviewed about church growth. The driving question of this interview was, "What were the real-life issues that you faced and overcame to grow the church"? I summed this up in seven integral real-life issues and hurdles I faced, and ultimately overcame when presented with the task of growing a new church.

I.
Real Life Issue:
Who's Coming?

The first real-life issue in launching Journey Church was "whose coming"? The biggest challenge before us was where would the members and worshipers come from. Having served as pastor in an established church with existing members, there was always the assumption that people would be present on Sunday morning. My previous church had an established history of over one hundred twenty five years, with members and worshipper faithfully attending each Sunday. The church was well known throughout the community and had a rich history and tradition. This was not the story for Journey Church. Journey did not have members and worshippers, and was not known throughout the community because it was new. A large part of our goal was to make Journey a household name, as well as a part of community conversations where people would talk about this new church that just started at the local gas station, supermarket, schools, or their workplace. Social media played a major role in making this happen.

In the early years, there was always an overriding fear, a lingering anxiety, that no one would show up.

Unfortunately, this was our reality on more than one occasion, where people actually did not show up.

◄ **The Outcome:** *Invite! Invite! Invite! The strategy was to be aggressive in our efforts to put people in the seats. This meant team accountability, as well as intentional evangelism. The entire team shared responsibility in inviting someone new on Sundays. This practice is known as "elbow evangelism." Our job was to essentially do "whatever it takes" to get people to come and see this new and exciting church called Journey.*

◄ **Growth Key:** *Everyone in the church must be committed to reaching new people.*

II.
Real Life Issue:
Stability

It was essential to have an adequate facility that would meet temporal needs while supporting the long-term goal. Hence, we journeyed through four different locations.

There were many advantages to not having a fixed location. Our "travels" allowed us to impact different communities with our ministry, and experience growth. Our launch team grew stronger and became resilient in its ability to overcome adversity. Flexibility was established early on, and has become ingrained in the DNA of Journey. As a ministry, we learned not to get fixated on the physical structure or location. Instead, we remained focused on the people that were coming, who enjoyed being a part of a new and different worship experience.

> ***When changing facilities and locations,***
> ***some people will not make the transition.***

One disadvantage of moving locations was losing those who focused on the physical structure, and losing patience with our process of development. Another disadvantage was having limited access to our rental space. *ie: middle school gymnasium, where journey called home for three and a half years.* Journey's largest growth spurt occurred while worshipping in the school gym. Needless to say, being in four different locations having to continuously make adjustments, A phrase was birthed that captured oak of these experiences.

"Carpet is cheap, but people are precious"

- ◄ **Outcome:** *As a result of limited access to the gymnasium, our team endured physical and mental fatigue with the weekly set-up and breakdown of the gym. It's no surprise that countless volunteer hours were necessary to prepare for approximately 450+ persons each week. This definitely was no small undertaking. Ultimately, we found that people were willing to be patient with us through our transition periods, and this, in turn, resulted in Journey thriving.*

- ◄ **Growth Key:** *Adversity produced strength and character.*

III.
Real Life Issue:
Being the New Kid on the Block

Quite honestly, there were times where we faced resistance and opposition. I don't know if the resistance was intentional or simply because we were the new kid on the block being introduced into the family. Sure, we had to overcome challenges such as, finding adequate meeting space, establishing a presence within the community, and staying focused on acting our age. We also recognized that as a new church, we didn't want to emulate existing ministries.

When we huddled during our weekly after action review, we came to the conclusion that, the same people we were looking for, were also looking for us. This kept our hope alive to continue doing what we were doing.

> ◄ **Outcome:** *It was obvious that Spiritual warfare was real in establishing Journey Church. Not everyone was excited as we were to see this new church take root within our Faith community. Although, it was eye opening, and sometimes hard to understand, it was necessary for us to experience this first hand. As a team and church, we understood what God was calling us to do. He was calling us to stand strong, push*

forward, and take our rightful place in spite of any resistance.

◄ **Growth Key:** *Everyone in a church plant must be aware of the possibility of external resistance and the reality of spiritual warfare. During these times, it was important and critical as a church that we remain focused on the main thing.*

IV.
Real Life Issue:
Impact on Family

This is very personal for me. Everyone comes into church planting with independent issues apart from the church. One challenge I faced was balancing the work of the church and caring for my parents who were in declining health. My mother was diagnosed with Multiple Sclerosis (MS), and my father was her caregiver. Shortly after my mother had succumbed to her battle with MS, my father's health was vastly declining. My wife and I, who were their primary caretakers at that time, were constantly managing the growth of Journey while being caregivers. Fortunately, I was blessed to have help from my siblings. It was a mental battle keeping my mind focused on growing when two of the people whom I loved so dearly were dying.

Another part of that family component was being a father of two young sons. At the time Journey was planted, my sons were entering elementary and middle school. It was important that I provide my sons with the proper attention, and nurturing they required during the formative years. Having grown up as the son of a minister, my father and mother were determined to defy the old stereotype of the preachers children being disobedient. Family values were instilled in my sisters and

I at a very young age, and it was important that I raise my children on those same values that molded me into the man I am today. Being raised by strong, loving parents, I was committed to ensuring my sons received that same nurturing love and attention that they needed from their father. However, I knew that starting a new church would require a lot of sacrifices. For a long time, I struggled with guilt as I constantly tried to juggle church, family time, school events, sports events, and the care of my parents. The struggle was real, as I had to depend heavily on my wife to ensure our boys would always have a parental presence and a sense of normalcy in their lives. The reality was…..I was nurturing my sons, but also birthing a church.

Although I continued to wrestle with the juggling of my time, I made it a priority to have my son's with me as often as I could on the journey. Seeing their father work passionately for the church would allow them to witness first hand what daddy was doing. Of course, they would let me know when they were bored and ready to go home. Little did I know that they were watching my every move, taking in everything they saw and heard. As they got older, they would play a significant role in the early stages of planting Journey Church. They were instrumental in countless families joining the church. They invited their friends, and of course, parents were interested in seeing why their children were up early, eager and ready to attend church. Their presence early on in the beginning stages allowed them to see how they could fit in and help daddy get people in the seats. Needless to say, this was "priceless"!

Additionally, as a husband, it was important that I make time for my marriage. In the early years I travelled a lot, so we had to be intentional about staying connected. There was always something to be done at the church. Looking back, I realize she didn't feel like staying late for meetings, coming to hang out to see the next order of steel delivered, or showing up for another Friday night setup when we were in worshipping in the gym. She had her own career as a special education teacher, and needed to focus on her job, as well as herself, which I understood. So, respecting each other's calling and working on a balance between birthing the church and our relationship was important and vital to sustain our marriage.

- **Outcome:** *Ultimately, making our church plant experience a "family affair" was a dual blessing. Many thanks to my children, and especially my wife who embraced the entire journey!*

- **Growth Key:** *The role of the spouse and family are valuable assets that must be nurtured along with the birthing of the church.*

V.
Real Life Issue:
Staffing

I remember when my wife had our first son. She was really apprehensive as to who she allowed to hold, feed, or touch him. For me, I would give him to anybody. Likewise, early on with Journey, I was truly fearful of not having the right people around me that I could trust. I didn't know who I could trust to come alongside me to ensure initial plans would be successful. Getting the right people on the bus was vital. Loyalty to the vision and the pastor had to exist for an effective launching.

The goal was to have staff who would be "Team Journey," willing to roll up their sleeves, and most important, have a teachable spirit. It's been my experience, not all the people who start off with you will remain with you. The ability to have a teachable spirit and to be willing to transition with the vision and ministry will contribute to longevity. Some people are with you for just a season.

- ◄ **Outcome:** *Dreamwork makes the team work!*

- ◄ **Growth Key:** *Everyone on staff is loyal to Christ, one another, and the vision/mission of the church. Honoring one another is key to* *loyalty. Fortunately, my first hires were two dedicated loyal servants to the ministry of Christ. One with a long military background and another who was fully committed to God in leading worship.*

VI.
Real Life Issue:
Establishing a Worship Culture

The worship leader played a critical role in this process. In this role she or he takes the stage to welcome, inspire, and invite people to come and make expressions of love to God. It was very important to have a band that could match the energy, was versatile in all styles of music and was in sync with the pastor. We exist in a community/society where people have options readily available with a simple stroke of their hand. In a world where technology has now taken over what was once considered traditional or normal means of living, we have Google, livestream, iTunes, Facebook Live, Instagram Live, as well as other social media outlets. With this in mind, we wanted our music to be at a level that would make people say, "I want to attend this worship experience"! Inspiring music often saved the day when the pastor was weary from a long and exhausting week. This is still true today.

- **Outcome:** *We created a worshipping culture that was unique and limitless, reaching people of all ages.*

- **Growth Key:** *Creating a worship experience that is not boring but relevant and fresh, has to be a top priority!*

VII.
Real Life Issue:
This is Not Your Grandmother's Church Anymore

My father was a pastor, and I remember being in seminary and coming home on the weekends. Dad and I would have long conversations about the church. He always shared good advice and wisdom, which he gained from over 55 years of pastoral experience in the African Methodist Episcopal Church (A.M.E.). I really miss those days.

Growing up, we went to church every Sunday, often literally spending all day at the church. I can remember my mother preparing sandwiches, and wrapping them in foil for us to eat if she knew we wouldn't make it home immediately after church. Sometimes those sandwiches would be left in the trunk of the car during extremely hot weather. Somehow, we never got sick from eating those sandwiches smothered in mayonnaise. Life was simple, and everything seemed to revolve around the church. Everyone knew where the church was even if they didn't necessarily belong or attend the church. Even the Easter Sunday church goer was familiar with many of the church's traditions. Sadly, those days have long passed away.

It seems the modern-day church is in direct competition with every area of interest in people's daily lives.

Expecting people to come to church out of obligation is quickly met with disappointment and frustration. It appears that the every Sunday Christian has disappeared, although being connected to that which is spiritual, is still important to many. This was very important for us to understand and embrace, because it helped us understand everything we did and needed to do to reach new people.

Getting interested in what was happening in the lives of people outside the doors of our church helped to connect us with the community. Being open to trying new ways of being the church brought new life. Holy experimenting, and establishing ministries that were indigenous to the people, sent a message that the church was current and relevant. Not being afraid to abandon activities that did not produce fruit was liberating. We were not afraid to make mistakes. We constantly evaluated and prayed over every plan and activity. A regular after-action review took place immediately following events, where we discussed what went well, what could have gone better, what didn't make sense, and what needed to be changed before the next event.

- **Outcome:** *We developed systems as an ongoing process to constantly evaluate and improve our church.*
- **Growth Key:** *Be open to what God is doing and join God in doing it!*

BONUS:
Let's Talk Money!

Often we shy away from talking about money in the church, which proves to be a big mistake. From day one Journey shared the vision of stewardship and embraced tithing as a goal for each member. Financial literacy classes are offered to help members understand budgeting and giving. Multiple online tools are used to allow easier access to giving.

Finally, Journey Church was blessed to have the financial support of the South Carolina United Methodist Church funding for new churches. Start up funding was critical to a successful launch. I am very grateful for them entrusting me to live out this God given vision. Journey continues to serve faithfully in returning support out of thankfulness for God's many blessings.

A Journey prayer:

"O Lord draw us to the people who need us and those who we will need to build your kingdom...AMEN

Final Word

Live without Fear! Plant a church as God calls. Grow your church as God calls. Journey in your personal and family life, as God calls, living without fear.

About the Author

Dr. George A. Ashford Jr. is a native of Columbia, South Carolina. A second-generation Methodist Minister, Dr. Ashford is the Lead Pastor of Journey United Methodist Church in Northeast Columbia. He received a Bachelor of Science in Marketing from South Carolina State University, a Master of Divinity from Gammon Theological Seminary, and a Doctor of Ministry from Columbia Theological Seminary in Atlanta, Georgia.

Dr. Ashford is married to Olisa, and they have two sons, George Adrian and Geordan Alexander.

www.ingramcontent.com/pod-product-compliance
Ingram Content Group UK Ltd.
Pitfield, Milton Keynes, MK11 3LW, UK
UKHW041944230426
12048UKWH00008B/125